WALKS IN SWALEDALE

HILLSIDE GUIDES

CIRCULAR WALKS IN THE YORKSHIRE DALES

- ④ WHARFEDALE
- ⑤ NIDDERDALE
- ⑥ CRAVEN DALES
- ⑧ WENSLEYDALE
- ⑩ WESTERN DALES
- ⑪ SWALEDALE

OTHER TITLES

- ① THE WESTMORLAND WAY - Appleby to Arnside
- ② THE FURNESS WAY - Arnside to Ravenglass
- ③ THE CUMBERLAND WAY - Ravenglass to Appleby
- ⑦ CLEVELAND WAY COMPANION - Helmsley to Filey
- ⑨ THE NORTH BOWLAND TRAVERSE - Slaidburn to Stainforth by David Johnson
- ⑫ WALKS IN BRONTE COUNTRY - South Pennines
- ⑬ WALKS ON THE NORTH YORK MOORS - WESTERN
- ⑭ WALKS ON THE NORTH YORK MOORS - SOUTHERN
- ⑮ WALKS ON THE NORTH YORK MOORS - NORTHERN
- ⑯ DALES WAY COMPANION - Ilkley to Bowness
- ⑰ WALKS IN CALDERDALE · South Pennines

WALKS
IN
SWALEDALE

by

Paul Hannon

HILLSIDE PUBLICATIONS

HILLSIDE PUBLICATIONS
11 Nessfield Grove
Exley Head
Keighley
West Yorkshire
BD22 6NU

First published 1987
3rd impression 1989

Cover illustration: Ivelet Bridge
Page 1: Calver Hill from Booze Moor

ISBN 1 870141 00 8

Printed in Great Britain by
Carnmor Print and Design
95/97 London Road
Preston
Lancashire
PR1 4BA

INTRODUCTION

The area explored in the pages of this guide is a very well defined one, being the valley of the River Swale from its beginnings in the tumbling becks of the wild Pennines to its departure from the Yorkshire Dales National Park near Richmond. Swaledale is the most northerly of Yorkshire's Dales and its remoteness from major centres of population has helped it remain relatively quiet and unchanged. Without insulting all of the other beautiful Dales valleys, it must be said that Swaledale is a little bit special.

Throughout its entire length the dale loses none of its grandeur, remaining steep-sided virtually all the way to Richmond. There is only one side-valley of any size, this being Arkengarthdale, the valley of Arkle Beck. It shares all the characteristics of the main dale. With its colourful, sweeping fellsides, there is a strong hint of lakeland in Swaledale.

This is walkers territory *par excellence*, the dale's attractions being largely of the natural variety from heather moors to the waterfalls of Keld, and inevitably back to the swift-flowing and often tree-lined river. The Pennine Way crosses the valley head and the Coast to Coast Walk treats its followers to the entire length of the dale. There are two distinct types of walking in Swaledale, the lush meadows and the mining-ravaged hillsides. These two aspects of the dale are its very trademark. No other dale in the park has a riverbank which can be followed so closely for such a distance, and no other has such an intense concentration of remains of the lead mining industry. Every corner of the dale displays the evidence, from the mines on the moors down through the gills with their smelt mills to the villages with their miners cottages. Many of the paths we follow lead up to the sites of former workings, which are slowly blending back into their hillsides. There is an impressiveness and even a certain beauty about these places which stem partly from an image of those hardy souls who, not that long ago, would walk several miles every day to slave away in these dark, damp holes.

The magnificent gateway to this glorious valley is Richmond, one of the finest little towns in the land. Its medieval charm and unrivalled character are a perfect match for the dale it guards. For those with transport it would make a reasonable base, but Reeth, the largest village, is far more satisfactorily situated in walking terms, with ample accommodation and several shops and inns.

THE ROAD NETWORK

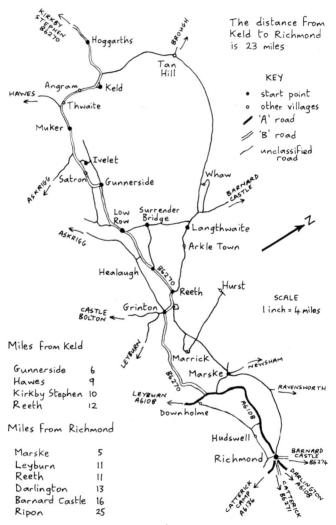

The distance from Keld to Richmond is 23 miles

KEY

- • start point
- ○ other villages
- 𝗹 'A' road
- ⫽ 'B' road
- ⫽ unclassified road

SCALE
1 inch = 4 miles

Miles from Keld

Gunnerside	6
Hawes	9
Kirkby Stephen	10
Reeth	12

Miles from Richmond

Marske	5
Leyburn	11
Reeth	11
Darlington	13
Barnard Castle	16
Ripon	25

As a bonus for readers who may have purchased companion guides, and also to celebrate completion of this Dales series, some extra walks have been squeezed into this guide. The 20 walks described range in length from 3½ to 11 miles, and all are circular. With an average distance of 5½ miles, they are ideally suited to half-day rambles. Each of the walks has its own chapter comprising of 'immediate impression' diagram, detailed narrative and strip-map, and notes and illustrations of features of interest along the way.

Although the strip-maps illustrating each walk should be capable of guiding one safely around, they serve no other purpose and are of course unable to show the features of the surrounding countryside. The simple remedy is an Ordnance Survey map, as follows:-

1:50,000 Landranger
sheet 92 : Barnard Castle
sheet 98 : Wensleydale and Upper Wharfedale
sheet 99 : Northallerton and Ripon
  (this map serves Walk 17 only)

1 inch to the mile
sheet 90: Wensleydale
sheet 91: Ripon

The Outdoor Leisure Map sheet 30 –
Yorkshire Dales Northern and Central areas
covers all but part of Walk 20 at the
larger scale of 1:25,000.

The area within this guide has no rail services, Richmond itself being the nearest they ever approached. Today one can still get as far as Darlington by train, from where it is a fairly short bus journey to Richmond. The adventurous could go one better and take the Settle-Carlisle line as far as Kirkby Stephen (assuming the service still exists) and then walk the 10 miles over Lamps Moss to Keld, surely an unrivalled way to enter Swaledale!

Overleaf are listed the various facilities which can be found in the area. Public transport takes the form of an infrequent bus service along the length of the valley from, inevitably, Richmond. On the 'inn-scene' there are several good village hostelries in the small handful we encounter west of Richmond, but outside Reeth traditional ale is not abundant.

SOME USEFUL FACILITIES

	Accommodation	Inn	Car park	Bus service	Post Office	other shop	Payphone	WC
Angram				✓			✓	
Grinton	✓	✓		✓	✓		✓	✓
Gunnerside	✓	✓	✓	✓	✓	✓	✓	✓
Healaugh				✓	✓		✓	
Hurst							✓	
Ivelet							✓	
Keld	✓			✓			✓	✓
Langthwaite	✓	✓			✓	✓	✓	✓
Low Row	✓	✓		✓	✓		✓	✓
Marrick	✓						✓	
Marske				✓			✓	
Muker	✓	✓		✓	✓	✓	✓	✓
Reeth	✓	✓	✓	✓	✓	✓	✓	✓
Richmond	✓	✓	✓	✓	✓	✓	✓	✓
Satron				✓			✓	
Thwaite	✓			✓		✓	✓	

There is a reasonable spread of accommodation from hotels down the scale to youth hostels. These can be found at Keld and at Grinton. There is camping near Keld and at a caravan site just west of Richmond.

SOME USEFUL ADDRESSES

Ramblers' Association
    1/5 Wandsworth Road, London SW8 2LJ
       Tel. 01-582 6878

Youth Hostels Association
    Trevelyan House, St. Albans, Herts. AL1 2DY
      Tel. St. Albans (0727) 55215

Yorkshire Dales National Park Office
    Colvend, Hebden Road, Grassington,
    Skipton, North Yorkshire BD23 5LB
      Tel. Grassington (0756) 752748

Yorkshire and Humberside Tourist Board
    312 Tadcaster Road, York YO2 2HF
      Tel. York (0904) 707961

    Tourist Information -
      Reeth - Swaledale Folk Museum
        Tel. Richmond (0748) 84373 (evenings)
      Richmond - Victoria Road
        Tel. Richmond (0748) 3525
        or in winter, Richmond 4221

Richmondshire Museum - Ryders Wynd, Richmond
      Tel. Richmond (0748) 3440

Georgian Theatre and Museum, Victoria Rd, Richmond
      Tel. Richmond (0748) 3021

Green Howard's Regimental Museum
    Trinity Church, Market Place, Richmond
      Tel. Richmond (0748) 2133

United Automobile Company
    Grange Road, Darlington, Co. Durham
      Tel. Darlington (0325) 65252

Yorkshire Dales Society
    152, Main Street, Addingham, Ilkley,
    West Yorkshire LS29 0LY

THE WALKS

Listed below are the 20 walks described,
the number being the key to easy location

THE WALKS

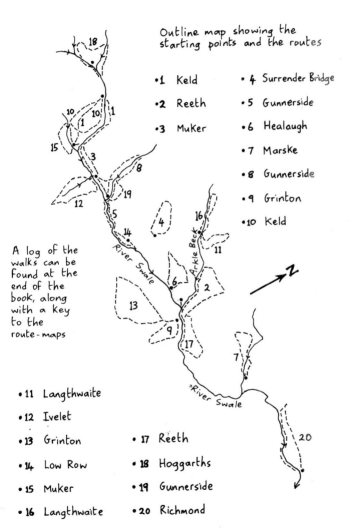

Outline map showing the
starting points and the routes

- 1 Keld
- 2 Reeth
- 3 Muker

- 4 Surrender Bridge
- 5 Gunnerside
- 6 Healaugh
- 7 Marske
- 8 Gunnerside
- 9 Grinton
- 10 Keld

A log of the
walks can be
found at the
end of the
book, along
with a key
to the
route-maps

- 11 Langthwaite
- 12 Ivelet
- 13 Grinton
- 14 Low Row
- 15 Muker
- 16 Langthwaite

- 17 Reeth
- 18 Hoggarths
- 19 Gunnerside
- 20 Richmond

11

WALK 1

6 miles

THE CORPSE ROAD AND THE SWALE GORGE

from Keld

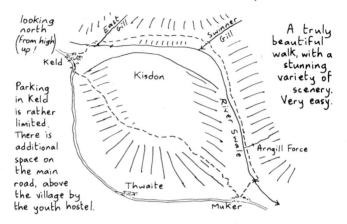

looking north (from high up!)

Keld

Parking in Keld is rather limited. There is additional space on the main road, above the village by the youth hostel.

A truly beautiful walk, with a stunning variety of scenery. Very easy.

THE WALK

Leave Keld by the lane up to the main road, and turn left along it for a couple of minutes until a rough track drops down to the left. This is the old corpse road, which will lead unerringly over the hill to Muker. On crossing a tiny beck it begins to climb, soon easing out and passing through several gates as it goes. Just beyond a short, walled section by some mining debris the summit of the track is reached, and a little down the other side the route of the Pennine Way is crossed as Kisdon Farm is seen across to the right. Continue down, briefly enclosed before joining the farm's access road. This well surfaced way takes us steeply down through the final two pastures to enter Muker along a short lane. Note the point of exit just to the left (signposted) on entering the village.

On leaving Muker take the stile by a gate at the 'rear' of the village – as mentioned above – and a well-defined path crosses seven fields linked by solid stiles to arrive at the riverbank. Turn right to another stile to follow the Swale the few yards down to Rampsholme Bridge. On the opposite bank drop down left to the river and soon a wide track is joined: it is accompanied almost all the way back to Keld. On crossing the first inflowing beck, be sure to stroll a short distance up its course to appreciate a charming waterfall.

Continuing by the river the track crosses a bridge below the ravine of Swinner Gill, then rises steeply before easing out above an increasingly impressive wooded, rocky gorge. This same track eventually descends to a farm bridge over East Gill - note the shared 'Pennine Way' and 'Coast to Coast' signpost-straight after which we take a left fork by East Gill Force to a footbridge over the Swale. From it take the path climbing right to a gate, and within minutes Keld is re-entered.

Lovely Seat
From Hooker
Mill Scar on
the Corpse road

Muker

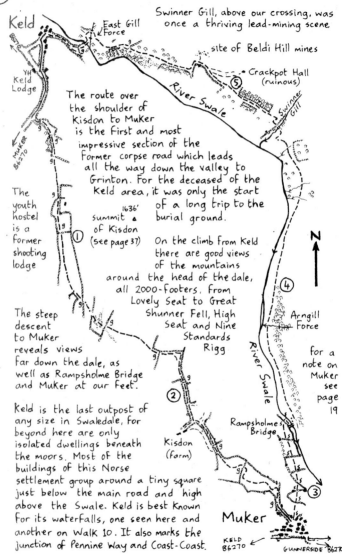

Keld

East Gill Force

Swinner Gill, above our crossing, was once a thriving lead-mining scene

site of Beldi Hill mines

Crackpot Hall (ruinous)

⑤

Swinner Gill

River Swale

YH Keld Lodge

MUKER B6270

The route over the shoulder of Kisdon to Muker is the first and most impressive section of the former corpse road which leads all the way down the valley to Grinton. For the deceased of the Keld area, it was only the start of a long trip to the burial ground.

1636' summit of Kisdon (see page 37)

The youth hostel is a former shooting lodge

①

On the climb from Keld there are good views of the mountains around the head of the dale, all 2000-footers, from Lovely Seat to Great Shunner Fell, High Seat and Nine Standards Rigg

N

The steep descent to Muker reveals views far down the dale, as well as Rampsholme Bridge and Muker at our feet.

④

Arngill Force

River Swale

for a note on Muker see page 19

②

Kisdon (farm)

Rampsholme Bridge

③

Keld is the last outpost of any size in Swaledale, for beyond here are only isolated dwellings beneath the moors. Most of the buildings of this Norse settlement group around a tiny square just below the main road and high above the Swale. Keld is best known for its waterfalls, one seen here and another on Walk 10. It also marks the junction of Pennine Way and Coast-Coast.

Muker

KELD B6270

GUNNERSIDE B6270

14

WALK 2

FREMINGTON EDGE AND ARKLE BECK

7¾ miles

from Reeth

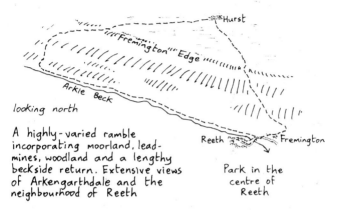

looking north

A highly-varied ramble incorporating moorland, lead-mines, woodland and a lengthy beckside return. Extensive views of Arkengarthdale and the neighbourhood of Reeth

Park in the centre of Reeth

THE WALK

Leave Reeth by the Richmond road, and immediately after crossing the bridge over Arkle Beck take a stile on the left. From the one just across to the right head ½-left across the next field to another stile, then follow the right-hand wall to a stile to empty onto a narrow lane in Fremington. Turn almost at once up the walled track to the left to join another narrow lane. Head left along this, ignoring a bridleway branching off and begin the long climb to Fremington Edge.

We remain on this lane throughout its course: at a gate it begins to deteriorate into a rough track, passing the aptly-named White House and continuing up to another gate. Only a little more climbing and the top is reached. From the gate in the wall along the top a wide track heads away, and leads unerringly across the moor towards Hurst, which comes into sight only on nearing it. Through a gate a prominent old chimney is passed before reaching the hamlet of Hurst.

Turn left along its lane which ends before two gates back onto the moor. Yet another wide track heads over it, taking us gradually up through a vast expanse of mining debris back towards Fremington Edge. After passing through a row of grouse butts the wall along the top appears. Here leave the track in favour of a gateway in a tiny angle of the wall.

15

With no path to follow now, head across to the scars of mining just ahead, keeping to the bottom side of them as far as possible. Continue on a generally level course with North Rake Hush prominent directly ahead across the side-valley of Slei Gill. As the gradient steepens bear round to the left, and a path should be located descending the slope to a gate. From it drop down by the wall to emerge onto a farm-lane by Strothwaite Hall. Turn left along it until it ends at the next farm, then head across two fields to near Arkle Beck at a footbridge.

Do not use the bridge but take the gate in front, beyond which our footpath breaks off the bridleway to remain nearer the beck. This it does for a good while before being deflected away from a bend in the beck by yellow blobs of paint on numerous trees. From here on the way avoids the beck for some time, crossing the fields by means of stiles in a near-straight line to arrive at a group of farm buildings.

Our route heads away in the same direction, with as many collapsed walls as intact ones. Beyond a long-since abandoned farm the beck is rejoined, but within yards the path forks and our choice is the good track branching left. This soon passes through a gateway and alongside a wall on the right. After two more intervening stiles, take one on the right, descending past a barn to two stiles in line. Follow a wall to another stile and continue on through two more fields. The latter and lengthier of these returns us to the road at Reeth Bridge, where we left the village.

For a note
on Reeth
see page 52

Reeth Bridge
is the
graceful
gateway
to the village
for those
travelling
up-dale.

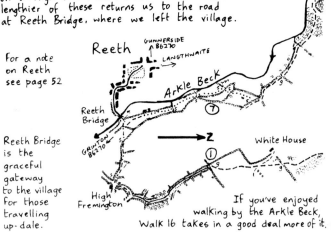

If you've enjoyed
walking by the Arkle Beck,
Walk 16 takes in a good deal more of it.

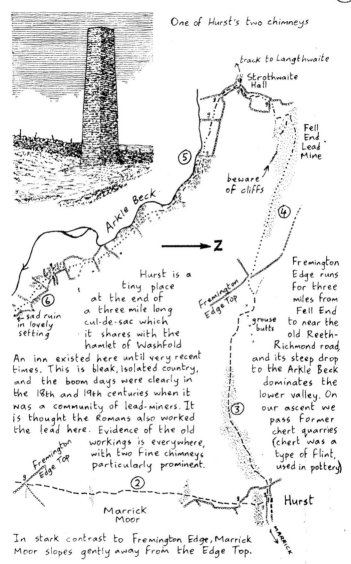

One of Hurst's two chimneys

track to Langthwaite

Strothwaite Hall

Fell End Lead Mine

⑤

beware of cliffs

Arkle Beck

④

→ Z

Fremington Edge Top

Fremington Edge runs for three miles from Fell End to near the old Reeth-Richmond road, and its steep drop to the Arkle Beck dominates the lower valley. On our ascent we pass former chert quarries (chert was a type of flint, used in pottery)

grouse butts

③

⑥

← sad ruin in lovely setting

Hurst is a tiny place at the end of a three mile long cul-de-sac which it shares with the hamlet of Washfold

An inn existed here until very recent times. This is bleak, isolated country, and the boom days were clearly in the 18th and 19th centuries when it was a community of lead-miners. It is thought the Romans also worked the lead here. Evidence of the old workings is everywhere, with two fine chimneys particularly prominent.

Fremington Edge Top

②

Marrick Moor

Hurst

MARRICK

In stark contrast to Fremington Edge, Marrick Moor slopes gently away from the Edge Top.

WALK 3

4¾ miles

THE SWALE BELOW MUKER

from Muker

looking north-west

Park in the village centre

Rampsholme Bridge

Calvert Houses

Muker

River Swale

Ivelet

Very easy walking
with good river scenery
and good views both up and down the dale

THE WALK

Leave Muker by a well-signposted stile by a gate between buildings at the 'rear' of the village, at the top of a short lane leading up to and behind the right of the post office. A well-defined path crosses seven fields linked by solid stiles to arrive at the riverbank. Turn right to another stile to follow the Swale downstream a few yards to Rampsholme Bridge. Just upstream on the opposite bank a wide track is joined and then followed to the right. It climbs a little and soon receives a tarred surface, but remains unenclosed and traffic-free to run parallel with the river all the way to a junction at Gunnerside Lodge. Turn right to descend to Ivelet.

Continue down the lane from Ivelet to the river, and just along to the right is Ivelet Bridge. Do not cross it, however, but take a gate on the right to accompany the Swale upstream. The way is straightforward, with an intermittent path staying close to the river after an early detour from its bank. After a long mile the path cuts out a bend in the river by means of a line of obvious gap-stiles in parallel walls, then rejoins the Swale for the last five minutes to Rampsholme Bridge. Re-cross it and retrace steps through the fields back to Muker.

Rampsholme Bridge

Rampsholme Bridge is a tall modern footbridge, and is the only crossing of the Swale between Keld and Ivelet Bridge. It is an excellent viewpoint for the lonely Swale gorge, as far upstream as the cleft of Swinner Gill.

The Farmers Arms, Muker

The path alongside the Swale witnesses some good river scenery as it flows over a wide, stony bed.

Muker is a good centre for the head of the dale, with accommodation, shops and an inn. The latter is the farthest up the valley, begging the pardon of Tan Hill, which at 1732 feet can in no way be said to be in a valley! Muker is also probably the most picturesque village in the dale, with a fine grouping of buildings rising above the beck. The river Swale rejoins the main road just below the village, after their enforced split by Kisdon.

Prominent in most views is St. Mary's church, which was first built in 1580 to relieve Grinton's load, taking off its hands the upper dale which then made Muker an extensive parish, in areal extent at least. The present structure dates largely from 1890. Other interesting buildings are the Literary Institute of 1868, and the school, with tablets proclaiming that the famous Kearton brothers of Thwaite were former pupils. Muker is also the venue for the Swaledale Agricultural Show in September.

WALK 4

GREAT PINSEAT AND HARD LEVEL GILL

5¾ miles

from Surrender Bridge

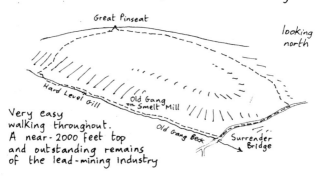

Very easy
walking throughout.
A near-2000 feet top
and outstanding remains
of the lead-mining industry

Surrender Bridge stands at the junction of two unfenced moor-roads, a mile north of Low Row, 2½ miles south of Langthwaite, and two miles west of Healaugh. It is named on O.S. 2½" maps but not on smaller scale maps. There are various parking spots.

THE WALK

From the bridge take the steeply-climbing road towards Langthwaite in Arkengarthdale. After the climb has subsided a wide track heads off to the left, and it leads unerringly and uneventfully up the moor. On levelling out Great Pinseat appears unspectacularly ahead, with a large sheepfold in front. Passing the fold, the track rises left to a cairn amidst mining spoil.

Only a couple of minutes across to the right is the wall running along the top of Great Pinseat, and a brief detour can be made to the highest point. The Ordnance column only appears as the wall is reached, for it is located just on the other side. Don't cross the wall to it — this gains nothing but involves a double-risk of damaging the wall.

Return to the track at the next area of spoil (again cairned), and the track now descends through a band of mining debris to reach a gate. From it the track accompanies Flincher Gill downstream, twice crossing it before passing Level House Bridge. Hard Level Gill leads down through the Old Gang smelt mill, and our track remains above the beck to return eventually to Surrender Bridge.

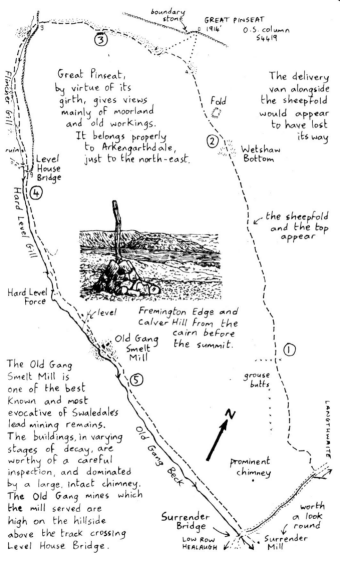

boundary stone

GREAT PINSEAT 1914'

O.S. column 54419

Great Pinseat, by virtue of its girth, gives views mainly of moorland and old workings. It belongs properly to Arkengarthdale, just to the north-east.

The delivery van alongside the sheepfold would appear to have lost its way

Flincher Gill

③

Fold

② Wetshaw Bottom

ruin

Level House Bridge

④

Hard Level Grill

the sheepfold and the top appear

Hard Level Force

level

Old Gang Smelt Mill

Fremington Edge and Calver Hill from the cairn before the summit.

The Old Gang Smelt Mill is one of the best known and most evocative of Swaledale's lead mining remains. The buildings, in varying stages of decay, are worthy of a careful inspection, and dominated by a large, intact chimney. The Old Gang mines which the mill served are high on the hillside above the track crossing Level House Bridge.

⑤

N

grouse butts

LANGTHWAITE

prominent chimney

Old Gang Beck

Surrender Bridge

LOW ROW HEALAUGH

worth a look round

Surrender Mill

21

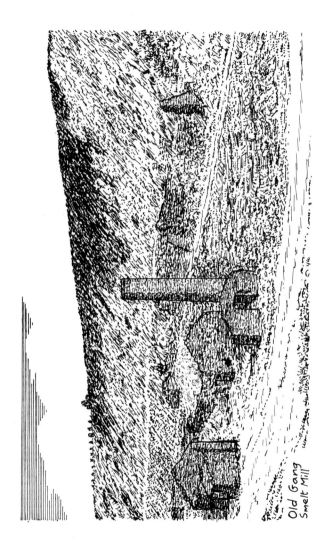

Old Gang
Smelt Mill

WALK 5

5 miles

THE BANKS OF THE SWALE

from Gunnerside

looking north

A simple, intimate riverside stroll

Gunnerside

River Swale

Isles Bridge

Park in the village

THE WALK

From the village centre take the up-dale road to the bridge over the Swale, and just beyond leave the road at a turn-off to Crackpot. This side road is also vacated straight after a cattle grid in favour of a track to the left. This is Dubbing Garth Lane, and is followed unfailingly down-river, generally sandwiched between an accompanying wall and the Swale itself. Eventually it becomes surfaced at a farm before reaching a T-junction. Turn left and soon left again to arrive at Isles Bridge.

continued across

For a note on Gunnerside see page 31

Gunnerside

Gunnerside New Bridge

MUKER B6270

CRACKPOT

Isles

Isles Bridge Lane

B6270

R. Swale

CRACKPOT

Haverdale House (Farm)

continued

Cross the bridge and take a stile on the left to commence a return to Gunnerside. An intermittent path soon fades, but keep close to the bank until near a barn, and from a stile behind it join the road as it approaches the river. When the road rises away, rejoin the river in the trees: soon a path materialises at a gate, then it clings to the Swale until the bank becomes steep and well-wooded.

Rise steeply to the right, twice crossing a collapsed wall to a gate back onto the road. It is left at once by the next gate, rejoining the riverbank to return to that first bridge. Just before it take a gate by a barn, and a series of stiles lead up through small fields to re-enter Gunnerside.

WALK 6

6¼ miles

from Healaugh

Calver Hill

looking east

There are several reasonable parking spots off the main road. Take care not to block any access.

Cringley Hill

Fore Gill Gate

Healaugh

A breezy circuit of a shapely hill, almost entirely on heather moorland

THE WALK

Leave the village by the up-dale Gunnerside road, and almost immediately turn right up a lesser road towards Kearton. This too is left at the first opportunity, up a drive to Thiernswood Hall. The track keeps left of the house to enter trees : at the end ignore the stile in front and take a gate on the right. In the wall-corner behind is a stile from where a track resumes to climb by the left-hand wall. Generally clear, it rises past the house at Nova Scotia to run below a walled enclosure to merge with another track. Now head up to the bottom side of another walled enclosure, and virtually pathless, head away from its far corner to pass above a fenced enclosure. Directly ahead the track reasserts itself while breasting the slope of Cringley Hill, and then remains clear to run undulatingly to arrive at the roadside at Fore Gill Gate.

Just before the gate, however, is a merging of tracks, and it is this other wide way we follow, now doubling back over the northern side of Cringley Hill. This infallible track eventually descends to join the road through Arkengarthdale. Turn right along its unfenced course for a good half-mile, then opposite a farm track a footpath sign points us back onto the moor. A path rises to a prominent sheepfold: here turn left along a very short-lived path, from whence a spot of heather-bashing takes over. All that is needed is to maintain a level course just beneath the markedly steeper slopes of Calver Hill.

Beyond a fenced fold a gentle rise leads to a fair length of wall on the brow of Riddings Rigg. Head away in the same direction as before, a track materialising to lead down

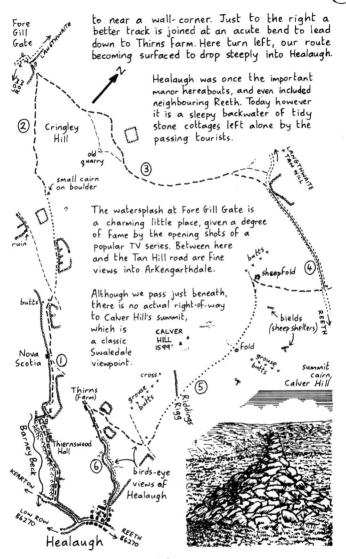

to near a wall-corner. Just to the right a better track is joined at an acute bend to lead down to Thirns Farm. Here turn left, our route becoming surfaced to drop steeply into Healaugh.

Healaugh was once the important manor hereabouts, and even included neighbouring Reeth. Today however it is a sleepy backwater of tidy stone cottages left alone by the passing tourists.

The watersplash at Fore Gill Gate is a charming little place, given a degree of fame by the opening shots of a popular TV series. Between here and the Tan Hill road are fine views into Arkengarthdale.

Although we pass just beneath, there is no actual right-of-way to Calver Hill's summit, which is a classic Swaledale viewpoint.

Fore Gill Gate

LANGTHWAITE

↓ 33 OR

② Cringley Hill

old quarry

③

small cairn on boulder

ruin

butts

Nova Scotia ①

Thirns (Farm)

Thiernswood Hall

Barney Beck

KEARTON

LOW ROW B6270

⑥

birds-eye views of Healaugh

REETH B6270

Healaugh

LANGTHWAITE TAN HILL ↗

butts

sheepfold ④

REETH

bields (sheep shelters)

CALVER HILL 1599'

Fold

grouse butts

summit cairn, Calver Hill

cross

grouse butts

⑤

Riddings Rigg

WALK 7
MARSKE BECK and SKELTON MOOR

6¼ miles

From Marske

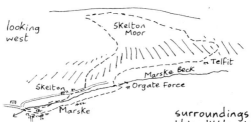

looking west

Skelton Moor

Telfit

Marske Beck

Skelton

Orgate Force

Marske

There is some parking by the post office, but the west side of the bridge offers better space

A splendid variety of surroundings is found in this little-known side valley, from woodland to moorland, and both of high quality

THE WALK

From the wide junction by the Post Office head along the lane branching off, continuing on the level when the lane turns uphill. Past a few cottages our way becomes a wide track, and a lovely woodland walk ensues. Avoid any branches up or down to arrive at a gate proclaiming 'OUT OF BOUNDS'. As this doesn't refer to us continue on to Orgate farm Just before the buildings descend a concrete farm-road to cross Marske Beck. A footbridge is provided, and Orgate Force can be seen a little upstream, although a brief foray up the right-hand bank will bring a more advantageous view.

Leave the beck by climbing the lane beyond, and at a lane-head by a large barn turn right on a level track which leads unerringly to Telfit farm. Keep left above the farm on a still-wide track climbing the hillside. It doubles back to a gate then follows a wall up to another gate. Now on Skelton Moor, go forward a few yards to a T-junction of tracks, and take the one going straight ahead. After passing an old fold, the Ordnance column atop the moor is reached, only a few yards off the track.

Back on the track keep on to a gate onto a lanehead, but instead of using it, turn sharp left on another track which links up with a wall to head back over the moor. Stay with the wall through a gate in an intervening wall, from where the valley of Marske Beck and our outward route appear far below. At the next gate the way become.

26

enclosed to drop down onto a lane.

Turn briefly to the right before taking a stile on the left after a small barn. Head diagonally across the field to a stile in a fence, then follow another fence away from it. When it turns left go straight on to drop to a stone bridge just past an old waterwheel. Cross it and follow the beck downstream using a gate into a short, wooded section before emerging at Marske Bridge.

Orgate Force

Marske Hall

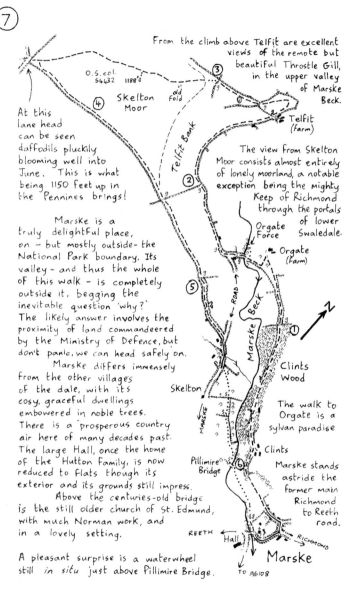

From the climb above Telfit are excellent views of the remote but beautiful Throstle Gill, in the upper valley of Marske Beck.

O.S. col. 54432 1188'd

Skelton Moor

④

old fold

③

Telfit Bank

Telfit (farm)

The view from Skelton Moor consists almost entirely of lonely moorland, a notable exception being the mighty Keep of Richmond through the portals of lower Swaledale.

At this lane head can be seen daffodils pluckily blooming well into June. This is what being 1150 feet up in the Pennines brings!

②

Orgate Force

Orgate (farm)

Marske is a truly delightful place, on — but mostly outside- the National Park boundary. Its valley - and thus the whole of this walk - is completely outside it, begging the inevitable question 'why?' The likely answer involves the proximity of land commandeered by the Ministry of Defence, but don't panic, we can head safely on.

⑤

ROAD

Marske Beck

N

①

Clints Wood

Marske differs immensely from the other villages of the dale, with its cosy, graceful dwellings embowered in noble trees. There is a prosperous country air here of many decades past. The large Hall, once the home of the Hutton Family, is now reduced to flats though its exterior and its grounds still impress.

Skelton

MARSKE

The walk to Orgate is a sylvan paradise

Clints

Pillimire Bridge

⑥

Above the centuries-old bridge is the still older church of St. Edmund, with much Norman work, and in a lovely setting.

Marske stands astride the former main Richmond to Reeth road.

REETH

Hall

RICHMOND

A pleasant surprise is a waterwheel still in situ just above Pillimire Bridge.

TO A6108

Marske

WALK 8   [GUNNERSIDE GILL]

6 miles   from Gunnerside

A fascinating exploration of this deeply-confined valley. The extensive remains of the lead-mines will stir the imagination. Overall, an absolute feast of colour.

Park in the village centre, by the bridge near the inn

THE WALK

     From the bridge by the inn in the village centre, take the wide track which follows the beck upstream. After being deflected round Gunnerside Hall the beck is rejoined and soon a path becomes clear to remain with it for a good while. On entering thicker trees a stile leads into a long sliver of woodland from where we rise high above the beck. The wood is vacated in dramatic fashion as we near the beck again, and after two close stiles a left-hand wall leads up-dale, taking in two more stiles to reach the beckside location of a former crushing mill.

     Keep left of the ruins to arrive at a stile, from where the path rises to another before continuing above the beck to reach – already – the last stile of the walk. From it a wide green track rises across the pasture before levelling out to run parallel with the beck, now far below. Soon an amazing scene of devastation greets the eye as an extensive lead-mining area is reached. Just beyond the last ruin in the immediate workings the path forks: take the left one down to the beck, which is followed up to Blakethwaite Smelt Mill.

     Amidst these ruins a large slab takes us over the beck, and after an exploration the inflowing Blind Gill is crossed with ease. This is the turning point of the walk, but a worthwhile detour is to follow the path up the west bank of Gunnerside Beck for a couple of hundred yards for a closer view of Blakethwaite Force.

     Back at the confluence a superb green way rises gently away from the beck, and this is the way to go.

Avoid any deviations and continue to rise to the last mining remains of the walk, where the track becomes level before it contours round Botcher Gill. Here we merge with a wide shooting-track, which beyond a gate commences a very gradual descent high above Gunnerside Gill.

When the track eventually curves sharply to the right, leave it and bear left across the open pasture on a broad spur. Soon the rooftops of Gunnerside appear below. Now descend a little more steeply to the right to join an unfenced road as it meets a cattle-grid to enter the village.

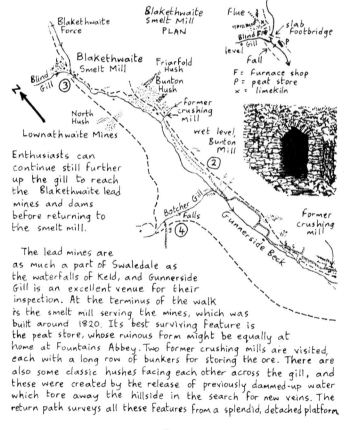

Blakethwaite Smelt Mill PLAN

Blakethwaite Force
Blakethwaite Smelt Mill
Friarfold Hush
Bunton Hush
former crushing mill
Blind Gill ③
North Hush
Lownathwaite Mines

Flue
slab Footbridge
Blind Gill
level Fall
F=Furnace shop
P=peat store
×=limekiln

wet level, Bunton Mill
②

former crushing mill

Botcher Gill Falls
④
Gunnerside Beck

Enthusiasts can continue still further up the gill to reach the Blakethwaite lead mines and dams before returning to the smelt mill.

The lead mines are as much a part of Swaledale as the waterfalls of Keld, and Gunnerside Gill is an excellent venue for their inspection. At the terminus of the walk is the smelt mill serving the mines, which was built around 1820. Its best surviving feature is the peat store, whose ruinous form might be equally at home at Fountains Abbey. Two former crushing mills are visited, each with a long row of bunkers for storing the ore. There are also some classic hushes facing each other across the gill, and these were created by the release of previously dammed-up water which tore away the hillside in the search for new veins. The return path surveys all these features from a splendid, detached platform

Blakethwaite
Smelt Mill

Gunnerside, like most of its neighbours, had its heyday in lead mining times, when it was a busy centre for the once-thriving industry. Again in common with neighbouring villages it is now a sleepy place. It was founded by the Norsemen, and it would appear that Gunnar was a Viking chieftain: until recently the inn sported a superb pictorial sign depicting the said invader.

The village stands astride its own beck, which apart from a level quarter-mile from here to the Swale, spends all of its time tumbling down the deep gill immediately above the village. Gunnerside Gill, even without its open air lead mining 'museum', is arguably the most impressive in the Dales. For virtually four miles its steep sides sweep uninterruptedly down to the beck, with scale and colour of lakeland proportions.

The mines, however, do add an extra element, and a gloomy day should be no deterrent to this walk. If anything, lingering cloud adds an almost tangible eeriness to the scene, assisted by the spirits of old miners, perhaps?

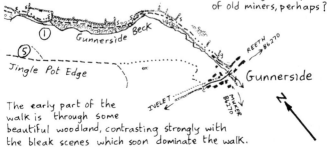

The early part of the walk is through some beautiful woodland, contrasting strongly with the bleak scenes which soon dominate the walk.

WALK 9 | COGDEN GILL AND GRINTON MOOR

4 miles — *from Grinton*

Some steep gradients, but easy
route-finding and
worthy objectives

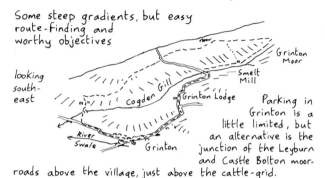

looking
south-
east

Parking in
Grinton is a
little limited, but
an alternative is the
junction of the Leyburn
and Castle Bolton moor-
roads above the village, just above the cattle-grid.

THE WALK

Leave Grinton by the lane climbing steeply from the
angle of the main road by the inn. After emerging onto the open
moor keep left at a fork, and the gradient finally fades as the
youth hostel is passed. Within a further half-mile the road bends
sharply to cross Cogden Gill. Take the track up the left bank to
soon arrive at the remains of Grinton Smelt Mill.

After an inspection there is a choice of routes to the
top of the highly conspicuous flue on the left. From the buildings
there are tracks up either side of the beck. When the one on the
opposite bank rejoins the main one, continue a little further to a
minor brow roughly level with the top of the flue. Now turn sharp
left to contour across the slope, possibly locating a very sketchy
trod through the heather. The site of the former chimney at the
flue top is soon reached. Anyone in a hurry could reach it even
sooner by simply following the flue up from the mill to its very
abrupt terminus.

From the flue top descend a few yards then swing
round to the right below the crags of Sharrow Hill. A green
track is joined which runs below the rocks then continues on
to meet the moor-road to Leyburn. Cross straight over to a
gate from where another pleasant track heads through two
pastures before descending to Cogden Hall. Keeping to the left
of most of the farm buildings and the hall, the access track is
joined to debouch onto the Richmond road. Turn left for the
final ten minutes back into Grinton.

Grinton, today a tiny village, was once the major centre for the dale above Richmond. A more curious feature is that it is the only settlement of any size on the south bank of the Swale. This no doubt stems from the south-facing slopes opposite seeing more of the sun. Grouped alongside the graceful bridge are the aptly-named inn and the church, which is known as the 'Cathedral of the Dales' because of its size. Until a chapel was established at Muker, Grinton parish was one of the largest in the land, extending westward through the entire valley as far as the Westmorland border.

As this was the only consecrated ground, the deceased of the upper dale had to be carried a long and arduous journey which we know today as the 'corpse road' (see Walk 1). The church itself is of Norman origin, but what we see is largely from the fifteenth century, being restored in the late nineteenth century.

Grinton is a good, honest Anglo-Saxon name, and nearby can be seen some of their strip lynchets, or cultivation terraces.

Grinton Lodge was built as a shooting lodge about 150 years ago. This castellated building is now a superbly-sited youth hostel with a panoramic view across the dale to Reeth, Calver Hill, Arkengarthdale and Fremington Edge.

Grinton Smelt Mill was built early in the nineteenth century, and operated for the best part of that century. It boasts two well-preserved buildings; the peat store and, by the beck, the mill with many interesting features. The flue is also excellently preserved.

Map features: River Swale, Grinton, lane, Good view of Marrick Priory's setting from just above Cogden Hall, RICHMOND B6270, Cogden Hall & farm, Cogden Gill, Grinton Lodge, REDMIRE, ③, ①, Worth a very short detour up the road is a splendid inscribed boundary stone by the roadside. Cogden Gill, Cogden Moor, Grinton Smelt Mill, flue, Sharrow Hill, LEYBURN, Grinton Moor, ②, N

Grinton Lodge
youth hostel

The old flue,
Grinton Smelt Mill

WALK 10

5½ miles

AROUND KISDON AND THWAITE

from Keld

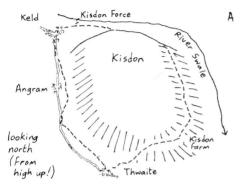

A circumnavigation of a colourful little fell with excellent views on the return from Thwaite to Keld

Park in the centre of Keld (if possible) or on the road at the top of the village

THE WALK

From the youth hostel head along the main road down the valley, and a little beyond a bridleway on the left a stile will be found. Here begins an invisible path through pleasant pastures, rendered easy to follow by punctuation by stiles at regular intervals. A good dozen are encountered, most being visible well in advance.

The road is rejoined after skirting the hamlet of Angram, and within a couple of minutes is vacated again at a stile on the left. Once more the path is but dots on the map, but the stiles again make life easy as we slope down to join a tiny beck. Thwaite is entered at the point where the Pennine Way departs it: after a look around and possibly a cuppa, return to this point. From here we trace the big daddy of the long distance paths back to Keld, and as a result the route-finding is made easy.

After two stiles our path strikes left through two fields to a bridge, then clings to the right of a field to climb to a stile at the top. A pleasant rise across a heathery slope ensues, continuing past a wall-corner to swing left up to another stile. Now with a wall on the left, go round to a gate, and then right alongside a wall to Kisdon farm.

Keep left of the farm to a gate, then take a walled track up to the left. When the wall parts company go straight ahead to join a track rising to the left. At a stile the way joins a near-level terrace which continues through many gateways and stiles and an occasional rash of stones. With trees now on the right and the path following the hillside round to the left, a gap in the accompanying wall is reached. Make use of it to descend to a junction of paths. Keld is but a few minutes along to the left, but for a short detour to see Kisdon Force, go to the right. Just down a slope is a gateway in the wall on the left, and from it a path goes down through the trees to a viewpoint for the waterfall. The descent to the very riverbank is somewhat steep.

To return to Keld rejoin the top path and go back along to the right, passing beneath tall cliffs before the way becomes enclosed to enter the village.

Kisdon Force

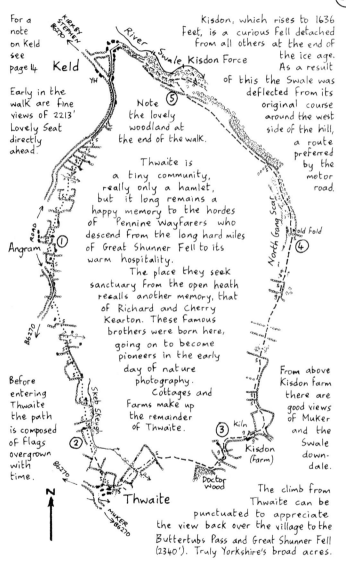

For a note on Keld see page 14

KIRKBY STEPHEN B6270

River Swale

Keld

YH

Kisdon Force

Kisdon, which rises to 1636 feet, is a curious fell detached from all others at the end of the ice age. As a result of this the Swale was deflected from its original course around the west side of the hill, a route preferred by the motor road.

Early in the walk are fine views of 2213' Lovely Seat directly ahead.

⑤

Note the lovely woodland at the end of the walk.

North Gang Scar

old Fold

④

ROAD

Angram ①

Thwaite is a tiny community, really only a hamlet, but it long remains a happy memory to the hordes of Pennine Wayfarers who descend from the long hard miles of Great Shunner Fell to its warm hospitality.

The place they seek sanctuary from the open heath recalls another memory, that of Richard and Cherry Kearton. These famous brothers were born here, going on to become pioneers in the early day of nature photography. Cottages and Farms make up the remainder of Thwaite.

B6270

Before entering Thwaite the path is composed of flags overgrown with time.

Skeb Skeugh

②

B6270

N

MUKER B6270

Thwaite

③ Kiln

Kisdon (farm)

Doctor Wood

From above Kisdon farm there are good views of Muker and the Swale downdale.

The climb from Thwaite can be punctuated to appreciate the view back over the village to the Buttertubs Pass and Great Shunner Fell (2340'). Truly Yorkshire's broad acres.

WALK 11

SLEI GILL AND BOOZE MOOR

5¾ miles

from Langthwaite

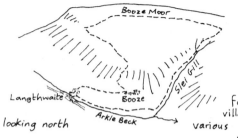

A fine combination of beck and moorland surrounds

Parking can be found in the tiny village centre or various locations on the road just above

looking north

THE WALK

Cross the bridge into the heart of the village and turn right immediately behind the first house. A wide track accompanies the beck downstream before striking away from it into a wood. At a fork keep left, rising out of the wood and crossing a field to a gate. Here leave the main track by taking the grassy path continuing straight on. It crosses several fields to reach the environs of the old lead mines of Slei Gill, and continues to rise as a superb green trod above the beck.

After a spell near the beck, a stone arch amidst more spoil is reached. Keep left of it to cross the by-now tiny beck just above it. Here it suddenly peters out : head directly away from the beck to cross an even smaller beck, continuing on to run parallel with a beck on the right (the right arm from the fork by the arch). At about the third grouse-butt leave the beck's environs and rise left to a prominent track. At a T-junction continue up to the left, rising a little before swinging left to drop past a wooden shooting box. At a fork beyond more butts, the left hand option is to be preferred : it rejoins the main track to arrive at a cairn overlooking the valley. Continue down to a sharp bend above a wall, and here leave it for the inviting track branching left. When it forks just before a wall, keep left to near another wall with a barn behind : a stile in the wall-corner takes us off the moor.

Descend to a gate at the field-bottom and turn left on a track down between crumbling walls. Continue through a gate, past a ruin and out onto the lane in Booze. Turn left for a glimpse into its privacy, and then back to the right to return unfailingly - and finally steeply - down into Langthwaite.

⑪

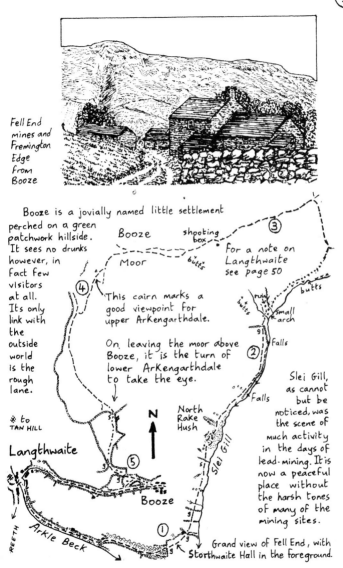

Fell End mines and Fremington Edge from Booze

Booze is a jovially named little settlement perched on a green patchwork hillside. It sees no drunks however, in fact few visitors at all. Its only link with the outside world is the rough lane.

Booze

Booze Moor

shooting box

③

butts

For a note on Langthwaite see page 50

butts

ruin

butts

small arch

④

This cairn marks a good viewpoint for upper Arkengarthdale.

On leaving the moor above Booze, it is the turn of lower Arkengarthdale to take the eye.

⚹ to TAN HILL

Langthwaite

⑤

N

North Rake Hush

②

falls

Falls

Slei Gill, as cannot but be noticed, was the scene of much activity in the days of lead-mining. It is now a peaceful place without the harsh tones of many of the mining sites.

Booze

REETH

Arkle Beck

①

Slei Gill

Falls

Grand view of Fell End, with Storthwaite Hall in the foreground.

39

WALK 12

6½ miles

A CIRCUIT OF OXNOP GILL

From Ivelet

Substantial gradients
Splendid views
Simple navigation

looking
south-east

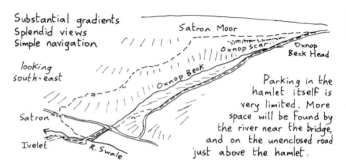

Parking in the hamlet itself is very limited. More space will be found by the river near the bridge, and on the unenclosed road just above the hamlet.

THE WALK

From the houses at Ivelet descend the lane to the river and cross Ivelet Bridge, then take a stile on the left to accompany the Swale downstream. On nearing a wall bear right to a stile, from where a short, steep path leads up to another stile. The next stile is just left of the barn in front, then cross the field to one just right of a barn. One more field takes us to the hamlet of Satron, with a short snicket leading onto the road just to the right.

Cross straight over to a narrow byway which begins its steep pull immediately. This well-surfaced way is beneath our feet all the way to Oxnop Beck Head. At the several forks avoid the lesser branches right to farms: fortunately the steeper parts are out of the way fairly soon. Eventually it completely levels out to run above the rim of Oxnop Scar before merging into the Muker to Askrigg moorland road just short of its highest point.

Double back to the right along the road to commence the long descent. As far as the cattle grid a good deal of the walking can be enjoyed on the grassy verges. When the road becomes enclosed remain on it for a further three-quarters of a mile before taking a gate on the right marked by a footpath sign. Descend the field to a stile left of a wood, then round the next field-bottom keeping above the trees. When a farm comes into sight below, drop steeply right to a stile right of a barn. Two fields are now crossed to a stile alongside Oxnop Bridge. Cross the road bridge then turn down a narrow lane to return to Ivelet Bridge.

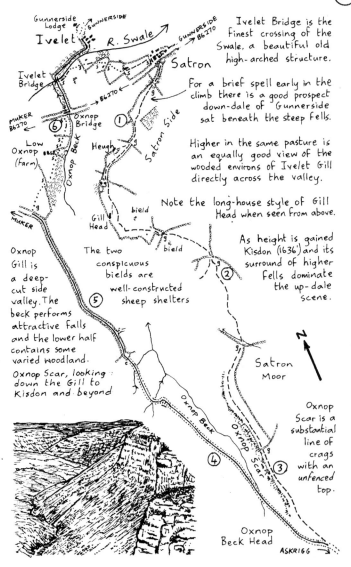

Ivelet Bridge is the finest crossing of the Swale, a beautiful old high-arched structure.

For a brief spell early in the climb there is a good prospect down-dale of Gunnerside sat beneath the steep fells.

Higher in the same pasture is an equally good view of the wooded environs of Ivelet Gill directly across the valley.

Note the long-house style of Gill Head when seen from above.

As height is gained Kisdon (1636') and its surround of higher fells dominate the up-dale scene.

The two conspicuous bields are well-constructed sheep shelters

Oxnop Gill is a deep-cut side valley. The beck performs attractive falls and the lower half contains some varied woodland.

Oxnop Scar, looking down the Gill to Kisdon and beyond

Oxnop Scar is a substantial line of crags with an unfenced top.

N

Gunnerside Lodge
Ivelet
GUNNERSIDE
R. Swale
GUNNERSIDE B6270
Satron
Ivelet Bridge
B6270
MUKER B6270
Oxnop Bridge
Satron Side
Low Oxnop (farm)
Oxnop Beck
Heugh
MUKER
Gill Head
bield
bield
Satron Moor
Oxnop Beck
Oxnop Scar
Oxnop Beck Head
ASKRIGG

WALK 13

HARKERSIDE MOOR AND APEDALE

11 miles

From Grinton

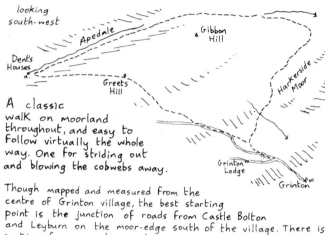

looking
south-west

Apedale

Gibbon Hill

Dent's Houses

Greets Hill

Harkerside Moor

A classic
walk on moorland
throughout, and easy to
follow virtually the whole
way. One for striding out
and blowing the cobwebs away.

Grinton Lodge

Grinton

Though mapped and measured from the
centre of Grinton village, the best starting
point is the junction of roads from Castle Bolton
and Leyburn on the moor-edge south of the village. There is
parking for several cars here.
This walk is also ideal for sojourners at the superbly
sited Grinton Lodge youth hostel.

THE WALK

From the junction opt for the right-hand fork (to
Castle Bolton) and after a few minutes climbing, a wide bridlepath
takes us off to the right. Beyond a fence a beck is crossed and the
track rises slowly towards Harker Hill. The track becomes briefly vague
in a grassy patch, but it continues straight on, crossing another wide
track and rising to become clear again and clearer still on merging
with another track. As a green strip it rises up through highly
conspicuous earthworks on the hill-top: from a guidepost there
we have a few faint yards to a cairn, then the track heads off
again on a level course across the moor.

At an area of old lead workings cross to the far
side of them and then follow the track's sketchy green downhill
course alongside the remains. As the track winds down it soon
becomes clear again, swinging left to join a wider track before
arriving at a large shooting-hut. Go through the gateway by it
and maintain a level course on what is now a narrower footpath.
At a fork of thin green strips take the right one to the foot of

a magnificent limekiln just beyond. Climb the slope after it to join the higher path and resume a level course past a cairn.

The path now begins its only real sketchy spell with the most imperceptible of rises, passing above a prominent large cairn and bending round to the left. On welcome return to more heathery surroundings the path becomes clear with a conspicuous shapely cairn a little ahead. From it the path continues to Birks Gill, rising past two grouse-butts before crossing above a tiny waterfall. Here the butts also cross the beck, but keep right of them and their peaty environs to rise to a cairn in front of a large spoil-heap.

A cairned track is followed left along a devastated strip to the moor-top. At the last cairn before the fence, bear right to a gateway with a large crater behind. From it a green track commences, first going left to another cairn then heading directly away from the fence. This is the head of Apedale, and the track is followed all the way down the valley to a crossroads of moorland tracks at Dent's Houses. Take the left arm which rises to Greets Hill, passing through an old fence on the top to commence what is positively the last leg of the journey.

The track descends away from the angle of fences, and on reaching lead mining remains it becomes unclear. Keep on the right side of the debris to join an unfenced moor-road. With its green verges it can be followed most pleasantly back down to the junction above Grinton, but a little alternative does exist: at the first bend go straight on down an almost hidden grass strip, crossing straight over a wide track and continuing down a path alongside grouse-butts to join another wide track. This is the one on which the walk began, and it soon rejoins the road just above the junction.

Greets Hill, looking across Apedale and Wensleydale to Penhill, Great Whernside and Buckden Pike

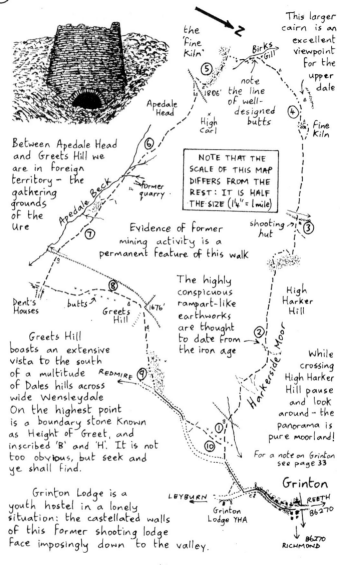

⑬

the 'Fine Kiln'

⑤

This larger cairn is an excellent viewpoint for the upper dale

Birks Gill

note the line of well-designed butts

Apedale Head

×1806'

×High Carl

④

Fine Kiln

Between Apedale Head and Greets Hill we are in foreign territory – the gathering grounds of the Ure

⑥

Apedale Beck

→ former quarry

NOTE THAT THE SCALE OF THIS MAP DIFFERS FROM THE REST: IT IS HALF THE SIZE (1¼" = 1 mile)

shooting hut

③

⑦

Evidence of former mining activity is a permanent feature of this walk

High Harker Hill

Dent's Houses

butts →

⑧

Greets Hill

×1676'

The highly conspicuous rampart-like earthworks are thought to date from the iron age

②

Harkerside Moor

While crossing High Harker Hill pause and look around – the panorama is pure moorland!

Greets Hill boasts an extensive vista to the south of a multitude of Dales hills across wide Wensleydale. On the highest point is a boundary stone known as Height of Greet, and inscribed 'B' and 'H'. It is not too obvious, but seek and ye shall find.

REDMIRE

⑨

For a note on Grinton see page 33

①

⑩

Grinton

LEYBURN

Grinton Lodge YHA

REETH
B6270

B6270
RICHMOND

Grinton Lodge is a youth hostel in a lonely situation: the castellated walls of this former shooting lodge face imposingly down to the valley.

44

WALK 14

THE ENVIRONS OF LOW ROW

3½ miles   From Low Row!

The attractive surroundings of Low Row include
a superb riverside
ramble

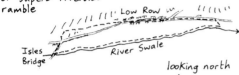

Park on or
just off the
roadside
by the
church
and inn

looking north

THE WALK

From the inn head along the road to Reeth for
ten minutes or so, and at a wood on the right look for a
footpath sign to Isles Bridge. Here a path descends to the
river and follows it upstream, clinging to its bank the whole
of the way to Isles Bridge. Turn up the road to a junction,
and only yards to the left climb an initially uninviting
grass slope.

When the trees and brief path subside, go right
along the top of a wall and a path returns,
meeting a wider track which in turn joins
the road through Low Row.
Almost at once the road
can be avoided by using
the large expanse of
grass alongside. It must
finally be
rejoined at
the former
school opposite
the post office,
from where the
inn is only
minutes
further.

This section
of riverbank,
even by Swaledale
standards, is sheer
pleasure: virtually the
entire length is lined
with attractive trees.

Low Row straddles the
main valley road for a good
mile, and incorporates the twin
hamlet of Feethams, a name still
seen on some maps. A long open
'green' runs parallel with the road.
The focal point is where the church
and inn are sited. The latter is an
imposing structure dating from 1638.

HEALAUGH
B6270

LANGTHWAITE

Low
Row,

River Swale

GUNNERSIDE B6270

Isles
Bridge

N

45

WALK 15

3½ miles

From Muker

Good views from low slopes, and two lovely villages

looking south

Park in the centre of Muker

Muker Side

Straw Beck

Muker

Usha Gap

Thwaite

THE WALK

Cross the bridge at the east end of the village and leave the road by an enclosed track rising slowly away to the right. The track soon doubles back to climb towards Muker Side. At a T-junction of walled tracks go right on a level section, and at the next junction turn sharp right to descend to a barn on a bend. Here vacate the imprisoning walls by a gate on the left. Cross two field-bottoms on a track passing an abandoned farm, and part way along the following field take a gate in the wall to slope down a field to a stile in the bottom-left corner. It leads to a footbridge after which a track runs out onto the road

If there is a reasonable amount of water in the lively Cliff Beck under the footbridge, then a very short detour is recommended. Take a stile just after the bridge and descend the field to a stile onto the road at Scar Houses. Walk only a few yards to the right to see a charming waterfall on the same beck, just above the road. Retrace steps along the road to meet the track and then continue past the Hawes junction before dropping down into Thwaite.

Turn along the short lane in front of the shop, and at the end a Pennine Way sign points the way through a short ginnel and a couple of stiles into a field. Here the Way strikes left, but we continue roughly parallel with a beck on a sketchy path across four fields to reach a tiny bridge over another beck coming in from the left. Cross the field-bottom beyond, head past a barn to a stile from where a short enclosed path joins the road at Usha Gap. Go left to the farm and up its drive to a stile on the right. Cross to a stile near the far corner of the field, from where a string of obvious stiles lead across a host of field-bottoms to enter Muker just behind the inn.

Thwaite

Thwaite

Thwaite

BKELD
B6270

(2)

Scar
Houses

HAWES

Falls

B6270

Usha
Gap
(farm)

Usha
Gap Bridge

(3)

For a note on Thwaite see page 37,
and For Muker, page 19

Flagged path
approaching Muker

Muker

B6270

Straw Beck

B6270
GUNNERSIDE

From the
slopes of
Muker Side
Great Shunner
Fell impresses
straight ahead,
while beyond
Muker is the
Swale gorge backed
by Rogan's Seat.

N

(1)

Muker Side

Three Loaning
End

'loaning'
means lane

WALK 16

5 miles

From Langthwaite

looking north-east

A valley walk with splendid
views of this relatively
little-known
side valley

Parking in the
village centre is limited,
but there are several other
places on the road above

THE WALK

Cross the bridge into the centre of Langthwaite
and leave by a track on the left just after the shop. From
a gate head across the field-bottom to a stile, then a sketchy
path crosses two more fields to a house. Follow its drive down
to join a wider drive, then head up it only a few yards to
locate a path through the trees. It soon emerges and two
field-bottoms precede a large meadow which is crossed parallel
with the beck to a stile onto a lane.

Cross straight over and up the lane opposite: this
quietest of byways is followed for a considerable time, soon
becoming unenclosed. It is vacated after a mile and a half
by a stile on the left shortly after a left fork near some
modern barns, and just before another farm. Four fields are
crossed in a direct descent, before a path zig-zags through
a colourful moor-like patch. On leaving it the minor lane
in Whaw is joined.

Go left to the bridge, and without crossing it
take a gate on the left and follow a farm-track through
three fields to approach the beck. A generally sketchy path
now continues through a number of fields and tree-lined
sections, always with a stile near to the beck. On eventual
arrival at a metal footbridge (having passed a wooden one
several pastures back) cross it and go downstream to a stile
onto a lane. Before taking the right-hand of the two gates
opposite, a short detour up the lane is recommended to see
a surviving powder-house, just over the wall on the right.

On returning to the gate a wide track leads
to another gate, where it turns left: just opposite a house

take a stile on the right. A short path joins a tarmac drive (the one to Scar House passed early in the walk) which is followed along its tree-lined way to emerge onto the road adjacent to the church. A left turn - complete with pavement - returns us through the rest of Langthwaite to the village centre.

The powder house,
C.B. smelt mill

St. Mary's, Langthwaite

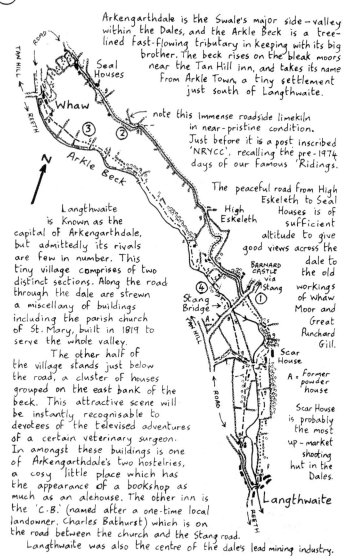

Arkengarthdale is the Swale's major side–valley within the Dales, and the Arkle Beck is a tree-lined fast-flowing tributary in keeping with its big brother. The beck rises on the bleak moors near the Tan Hill inn, and takes its name from Arkle Town, a tiny settlement just south of Langthwaite.

ROAD

TAN HILL ROAD

Seal Houses

REETH

Whaw

③ ②

Arkle Beck

N

note this immense roadside limekiln in near-pristine condition. Just before it is a post inscribed 'NRYCC', recalling the pre-1974 days of our famous 'Ridings.

High Eskeleth

The peaceful road from High Eskeleth to Seal Houses is of sufficient altitude to give good views across the dale to the old workings of Whaw Moor and Great Punchard Gill.

BARNARD CASTLE via Stang

④ ①

Stang Bridge →

A.

TAN HILL

ROAD

Scar House

A = former powder house

Scar House is probably the most up-market shooting hut in the Dales.

Langthwaite

REETH

Langthwaite is known as the capital of Arkengarthdale, but admittedly its rivals are few in number. This tiny village comprises of two distinct sections. Along the road through the dale are strewn a miscellany of buildings including the parish church of St. Mary, built in 1819 to serve the whole valley.

The other half of the village stands just below the road, a cluster of houses grouped on the east bank of the beck. This attractive scene will be instantly recognisable to devotees of the televised adventures of a certain veterinary surgeon. In amongst these buildings is one of Arkengarthdale's two hostelries, a cosy little place which has the appearance of a bookshop as much as an alehouse. The other inn is the 'C.B.' (named after a one-time local landowner, Charles Bathurst) which is on the road between the church and the Stang road.

Langthwaite was also the centre of the dale's lead mining industry.

WALK 17 | MARRICK PRIORY AND THE SWALE

6 miles   *from Reeth*

Easy walking with good lower
valley scenery and surprise
distant views on the return

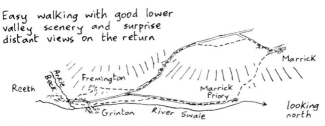

Park in the centre of Reeth

THE WALK

Leave Reeth by the Richmond road, and a little after crossing the bridge over Arkle Beck take a wicket-gate on the right. After leaving some farm buildings behind, our path short-cuts the beck's confluence with the Swale and bears to the left, round a wall-corner to a wicket-gate and then straight ahead to a gate by Grinton Bridge. Cross straight over the road and a footpath clings to the riverbank until a stile admits onto a fenced lane. Turn right along this quiet byway to Marrick Priory, whose tower will have been in sight for quite some time.

At a cattle-grid by the priory the lane becomes a farm-track: here leave it and climb a path to the left to enter a wood. A marvellous flagged path heads up through it, and on leaving the wood remain with the right-hand wall as a sketchy path becomes a wide track to enter Marrick itself. At the first junction turn left up onto the through road, and then go left along it past a farm.

Soon after a small dip in the road look for a stile on the left, and follow a wall away. At a stile cross to the wall's other side and stay with it through several intervening stiles to join a road. A steep descent of this quiet lane ensues until just beyond a bend by a track to West Hag, a stile leads off to the right to begin the last lap. This consists of an invisible field-path which runs a level course making use of stiles and gateways and presenting no problems.

Fremington is reached when a narrow, enclosed path is joined just after an enclosed 'green lane' is crossed at right-angles. Head along the footpath onto a narrow lane,

51

following it left and then right at the first opportunity. When it swings left to descend steeply, go straight along a track to a stile. A path accompanies a left-hand wall through a gateway to a stile, then heads half-right across the next field to a stile beyond which the final stile empties onto a road. Turn right to cross the bridge and re-enter Reeth.

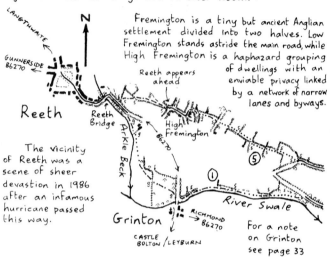

Fremington is a tiny but ancient Anglian settlement divided into two halves. Low Fremington stands astride the main road, while High Fremington is a haphazard grouping of dwellings with an enviable privacy linked by a network of narrow lanes and byways.

The vicinity of Reeth was a scene of sheer devastion in 1986 after an infamous hurricane passed this way.

For a note on Grinton see page 33

Reeth is popularly known as the capital of upper Swaledale, in effect the whole of that part of the dale within the National Park boundary. It boasts an enviable position on the lower slopes of Calver Hill, well above the Swale and the Arkle Beck. It is actually the latter of these two watercourses to which it shows allegiance, with neighbouring Grinton claiming the Swale. The village centrepiece is a large, sloping green, with the main buildings stood back on all sides.

There is a confident air about this one-time market town which radiates chiefly from the hoary inns and the shops alongside the green. Reeth caters indiscriminantly for dalesfolk and visitors alike, and is the ideal centre for a stay in the valley. Unfortunately parking limitations result in an untidy scene around the green in summer months. Inextricably linked with the lead mining days, Reeth was once much more populous. There is an absorbing folk museum here, while annual agricultural shows and festivals add to its local cultural attractions.

Marrick
Priory

✻ The top of the road is an excellent viewpoint, the setting of Reeth under Calver Hill being particularly well-displayed.
Also well seen on the descent is Grinton, with its isolated youth hostel at Grinton Lodge high on the moor above the village.

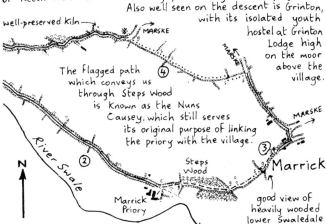

well-preserved kiln

The flagged path which conveys us through Steps Wood is known as the Nuns Causey, which still serves its original purpose of linking the priory with the village.

good view of heavily wooded lower Swaledale

Marrick Priory,
in its pastoral riverside setting was founded early in the twelfth century to house Benedictine nuns, and the larger part of the remains have been converted into a residential youth activity centre. Access is restricted to a gaze round the exterior. Marrick village stands high above at a breezy thousand feet up, and its better times were in the heyday of lead mining.

WALK 18

5½ miles

BIRKDALE AND WHITSUNDALE

From Hoggarths

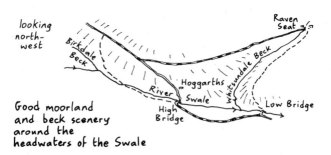

looking
north-
west

Good moorland
and beck scenery
around the
headwaters of the Swale

The farm of Hoggarths is a good mile past the Tan Hill junction
west of Keld. There is parking for several cars just after the
road crosses the Swale before climbing to the farm.

THE WALK

From the Keld side of the bridge (High Bridge) take
the track running upstream, and just through a gate fork to
the left between a stream and a wall. At a barn take a gate
to its right and continue on a level course, soon leaving a wall
behind and joining the beckside. Follow it to a stone arched
bridge and then resume up the opposite bank. After having
been deflected by trees up to a gate, go on to join a track
at an assortment of buildings at Firs.

Take the track to maintain our upstream course, but
when it swings left to become enclosed, continue along another
track alongside the left-hand wall. It soon rises above the wall
to suddenly end: bear left, nearing the wall again to a stile
at the far end. From it climb half-right to an old cottage,
and then follow its access track up to a gate. Once through,
leave the track and accompany the wall to the left. A little
up to the right is the unfenced B6270 road, and when the wall
nears it climb to join it in the vicinity of a footpath sign.

Now turn right along the road - or its attendant
verge - and within a few minutes a minor junction is reached.
Here turn left along the peaceful and largely unfenced access
road to its destination and terminus, Raven Seat. Enter the
hamlet by a stone arched bridge then turn right up into a

54

farmyard. Take a gate in the right-hand wall and then head downstream, parallel with Whitsundale Beck through several fields.

From a gate just beyond an attractive waterfall, climb half-left to a barn, continuing on a now-level course through several more pastures. Beyond a gate in a fence the path forks: take the right one to pass along the bottom side of a large crumbling enclosure. At a guidepost beyond continue on a level sheeptrod to avoid wet ground by the barns below, then descend to a gate at the next wall junction. A good track then drops down past a farm and over the Swale at Low Bridge to rejoin the B6270 Keld - Kirkby Stephen road.

Now turn right for a steady ten minutes along the road back to the next bridge, which is where the walk began.

Raven Seat is a tiny farming hamlet more than a little off the beaten track.

Unfortunately there is no public right-of-way to lonely Birkdale Tarn just above the road.

Hill Top From the path one can gaze down into the deep wooded gorge of Oven Mouth.

The River Swale is formed by the meeting of Birkdale Beck and Great Sleddale Beck, and consequently our first mile is also the first mile of the Swale.

Whitsundale Beck is the first major tributary, the confluence being seen to good advantage from the road above, just before the walk ends.

55

WALK 19　　　　| THE ENVIRONS OF GUNNERSIDE |

5 miles　　　　　　　　　　　　From Gunnerside

A walk of immense variety: lush meadows, high tracks
and lead-mining remains.
Marvellous views of　　　　　　　　　　　　　　looking
the main valley and　　　　　　　　　　　　　north-west
Gunnerside Gill

Park in
the village
centre

THE WALK

　　　　From the bridge in the village centre, depart along the
lane to the right of the main up-dale road: it is identifiable by
the tidy little green at the start of it. The lane soon ends at
the school, and a gate to its right leads between modern housing
to a gate into a field. The way now heads across countless meadows
keeping generally level to arrive at a beck, crossing it by a tiny
footbridge to emerge into the hamlet of Ivelet.

　　　　At the lane turn up to the right, bearing right at
a junction, crossing a bridge and finally becoming level at the
open hillside. After a short while take a wide track branching up
to the left. It rises around the hill high above Gunnerside Gill,
and though it can be seen climbing far ahead, we leave it at the
first opportunity when a lesser track forks right to slope steadily
down to the beck. On the opposite bank are the remains of lead
workings, and a little further upstream cross the beck at a still-
tall ruin on our bank. Just behind a smaller ruin over the beck,
the main path up the gill is joined at a stile.

　　　　From the stile the path rises away from the beck,
but before reaching a wall-corner turn right at a crossroads
to begin the return to Gunnerside. The new path becomes sketchy
as it rises to a narrow stile below a low ruin. Continue across
the tops of two fields, emerging past a tiny section of wall and
on to a wall-corner. Keep well above the wall and a path appears
before joining a wide green track.

　　　　After going through a gateway the track passes
several groups of farm buildings, and remains fairly level before
meeting another track at a gate on the right. With Gunnerside far
below, go through the gate and accompany this gentle byway on
its steep but highly enjoyable descent back into the village.

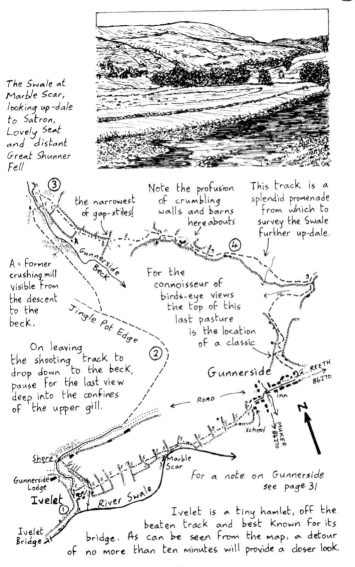

The Swale at Marble Scar, looking up-dale to Satron, Lovely Seat and distant Great Shunner Fell

the narrowest of gap-stiles!

Note the profusion of crumbling walls and barns hereabouts

This track is a splendid promenade from which to survey the Swale further up-dale.

③

Gunnerside Beck

④

A = former crushing mill visible from the descent to the beck.

Jingle Pot Edge

For the connoisseur of birds-eye views the top of this last pasture is the location of a classic

On leaving the shooting track to drop down to the beck, pause for the last view deep into the confines of the upper gill.

②

Gunnerside

REETH B6270

ROAD

Inn

N

school

MUKER B6270

Shore

Gill

Marble Scar

For a note on Gunnerside see page 31

Gunnerside Lodge

Ivelet

①

River Swale

Ivelet Bridge

Ivelet is a tiny hamlet, off the beaten track and best known for its bridge. As can be seen from the map, a detour of no more than ten minutes will provide a closer look.

WALK 20

7½ miles

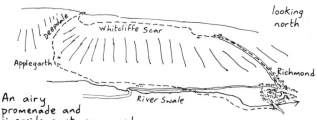

WHITCLIFFE SCAR AND THE SWALE

from Richmond

looking north

Deepdale

Whitcliffe Scar

Applegarth

Richmond

River Swale

An airy
promenade and
riverside pastures provide
scenery as varied as
anywhere further up-dale

The centre of Richmond
has ample car-parking

THE WALK

Leave the top end of the Market Place along Finkle Street, turning left along Newbiggin and right along Cravengate. A little further on the road swings left, and here leave it by a long avenue, Westfields, rising straight ahead. It leaves the houses to become a quiet lane, remaining surfaced as far as Whitcliffe farm. Now a track, remain on it until level with a farm on the left, and then climb the steep field to a fence at the top. Go left with it, up through a gateway, and then veer left to a fence running along the top of the eastern end of Whitcliffe Scar.

At an intervening wall we are conveyed to the scar side of the fence, and here we remain to reach the monument at Willance's Leap. Keep company with what is now a wall on the right, and our level path swings round with it, still above the Scar and then above a farm road in Deepdale. Eventually it is joined at its junction with a road, and we double back down the farm road as far as a cattle grid just short of East Applegarth. Take a stile just before it and descend by a well-collapsed wall, skirting the confines of Low Applegarth to a stile and gate in a fence. Just below it go left through a gateway, descending half-left through a gap in a wall, and similarly through a larger pasture to join a fence on the left. Passing a ruined barn continue down to a stile and thence onto the riverbank.

Two lengthy riverside pastures ensue, and although in neither does the unclear right of way appear to cling to the river, it seems more sensible and pleasant than to wander through the centre of the fields in aimless fashion. At the end of the second

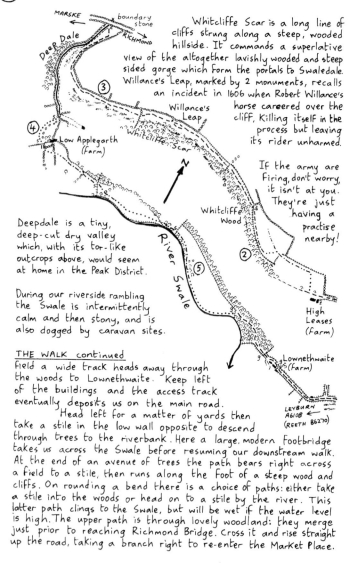

MARSKE ← ....× boundary stone
Deep Dale
RICHMOND
(3)
Willance's Leap
(4)
Low Applegarth (Farm)
Whitcliffe Scar
N ↑
Whitcliffe Wood
River Swale
(2)
(5)
High Leases (Farm)
Lownethwaite (Farm)
LEYBURN A6108 ←
(REETH B6270)

Whitcliffe Scar is a long line of cliffs strung along a steep, wooded hillside. It commands a superlative view of the altogether lavishly wooded and steep sided gorge which form the portals to Swaledale. Willance's Leap, marked by 2 monuments, recalls an incident in 1606 when Robert Willance's horse careered over the cliff, killing itself in the process but leaving its rider unharmed.

If the army are firing, don't worry, it isn't at you. They're just having a practise nearby!

Deepdale is a tiny, deep-cut dry valley which, with its tor-like outcrops above, would seem at home in the Peak District.

During our riverside rambling the Swale is intermittently calm and then stony, and is also dogged by caravan sites.

THE WALK continued

Field a wide track heads away through the woods to Lownethwaite. Keep left of the buildings and the access track eventually deposits us on the main road.
    Head left for a matter of yards then take a stile in the low wall opposite to descend through trees to the riverbank. Here a large, modern footbridge takes us across the Swale before resuming our downstream walk. At the end of an avenue of trees the path bears right across a field to a stile, then runs along the foot of a steep wood and cliffs. On rounding a bend there is a choice of paths: either take a stile into the woods or head on to a stile by the river. This latter path clings to the Swale, but will be wet if the water level is high. The upper path is through lovely woodland: they merge just prior to reaching Richmond Bridge. Cross it and rise straight up the road, taking a branch right to re-enter the Market Place.

Richmond is the gateway to Swaledale, although passing through it is the last thing to do. This is a truly remarkable town, steeped in history and retaining so much of its past, where other, less remote places have succumbed to the 20th century. Dominating the town is the castle, which stands on a rocky promontory high above the Swale. It was begun in 1071 by Alan Rufus, and the well-preserved ruins are now in the care of English Heritage and open to the public. Outstanding is the enormous 12th century keep, which watches over the whole town including, almost at its feet, the Market Place.

This equally-enormous feature shares double-bill with the castle, and has a multitude of uses. In the centre of its sloping cobbles is the church of the Holy Trinity with its 14th century tower. The building uniquely incorporates a row of shops, and houses the Green Howards Museum. Lined by shops and inns the Market Place is also used as a bus station as well as for its original purpose on Saturdays. A market cross is still very much in evidence.

Outside of the square, from which numerous wynds (narrow ways) radiate, is the parish church of St. Mary which includes a 14th century tower and 16th century stalls. Also in the vicinity is the impressively upstanding Grey Friars Tower, across the road from the Georgian Theatre. This fascinating place dates from 1788, and having been restored in the 1960's it now serves its original function once more.

The presence of the military around the town is due to the proximity of Catterick Camp. Also nearby are the Premonstratensian remains of Easby Abbey, dating from 1152.

If you've sampled this scenery on a good day, you may be surprised to discover you haven't set foot in the National Park.

The wooded eminence of Round Howe and much of the woodland in the vicinity is in the hands of the National Trust.

LOG OF THE WALKS

These two pages provide an opportunity to maintain a permanent record of the walks completed

WALK	DATE	TIME Start	TIME Finish	WEATHER	COMMENTS
1					
2					
3					
4					
5					
6					
7					
8					

1	
10	
11	
12	
13	
14	
15	
16	
17	
18	
19	
20	

KEY TO THE MAP SYMBOLS

direction of north

scale
2½ inches = 1 mile

Route — clear — sketchy ⋯ no visible path

Route on public road — unenclosed / wall / fence/hedge

River/beck — bridge

Marsh

Peat grough

Crags

Limestone clints

Loose rocks/scree

Cairns
summit   other

Trees

Buildings

Church

Abbreviations
c = cattle grid
s = stile
g = gate

Miles from start
③

THE COUNTRY CODE

Respect the life and work of the countryside
Protect wildlife, plants and trees
Keep to public paths across farmland
Safeguard water supplies
Go carefully on country roads
Keep dogs under control
Guard against all risks of fire
Fasten all gates
Leave no litter - take it with you
Make no unnecessary noise
Leave livestock, crops and machinery alone
Use gates and stiles to cross fences, hedges and walls